W9-CBH-525

BLAZERS

WEAPONS OF WAR

WEAPONS OF THE

CIVIL WAR

by Matt Doeden

Reading Consultant:
Barbara J. Fox
Reading Specialist
North Carolina State University

Content Consultant:
Tim Solie
Adjunct Professor of History
Minnesota State University, Mankato

Capstone
press

Mankato, Minnesota

Blazers is published by Capstone Press,
151 Good Counsel Drive, P.O. Box 669, Mankato, Minnesota 56002.
www.capstonepress.com

Library of Congress Cataloging-in-Publication Data
Doeden, Matt.
    Weapons of the Civil War / by Matt Doeden.
    p. cm. — (Blazers. Weapons of war)
    Includes bibliographical references and index.
    ISBN-13: 978-1-4296-1968-4 (hardcover)
    ISBN-10: 1-4296-1968-6 (hardcover)
    1. United States — History — Civil War, 1861–1865 — Equipment and
supplies — Juvenile literature. 2. Military weapons — United States — History
— 19th century — Juvenile literature. I. Title.
U818.D64 2009
623.40973'09034 — dc22   2008000526

Summary: Describes the weapons of the Civil War, including small arms and
larger weapons.

Editorial Credits

Mandy Robbins, editor; Alison Thiele, designer; Kyle Grenz, production designer;
    Jo Miller, photo researcher

Photo Credits

Alamy/North Wind Picture Archives, 10 (bottom); Corbis, 19; Getty Images Inc./
Hulton Archive, 5, 6; Getty Images Inc./Hulton Archive/J. F. Gibson, 22; Getty
Images Inc./Stock Montage, 15, 28; The Granger Collection, New York, 17 (cutlass);
iStockphoto/Jason Lugo, 25 (Ordinance rifle); James P. Rowan, 13 (both), 16 (Colt
revolver, LaMat revolver, Spencer repeating rifle), 17 (saber, Springfield rifle), 24
(12-pound cannon, 32-pound cannon, Parrot rifle), 25 (13-inch mortar); Library of
Congress, 9; The Image Works/The Board of Trustees of the Armouries/Heritage-
Images, cover (both), 10–11 (top), 21, 25 (Gatling gun); The Image Works/US
National Archives/Roger-Viollet, 27; Shutterstock/Marilyn Volan (grunge background
elements), all; www.historicalimagebank.com, 25 (cannonball, grenade)

1 2 3 4 5 6 13 12 11 10 09 08

TABLE OF CONTENTS

A NATION DIVIDED

The boom of cannons fills the air. Soldiers fall to the ground during a bloody Civil War (1861–1865) battle.

WEAPON FACT

During the Civil War, the Northern states were called the Union. The Southern states were called the Confederacy.

The Civil War was a dark time in U.S. history. The Northern and Southern states had different views about **slavery** and states' rights. The two sides fought each other with powerful weapons.

slavery — the act of owning other people

WEAPON FACT

The first battle of the Civil War was the battle of Fort Sumter. Not one person died in that battle.

RIFLES, REVOLVERS, AND BLADES

Civil War soldiers carried rifles. These long guns had to be reloaded after every shot. Northern soldiers carried the 1861 Springfield. It had good **range** but was slow to load.

range — the distance that a bullet can travel

Union soldier with rifle

Whitworth rifle

Southern soldiers fired
Whitworth rifles. These guns
fired long bullets with six sides.

WEAPON FACT

Skilled riflemen could pick off enemies more
than 1,000 feet (305 meters) away.

Some soldiers also used small guns called revolvers. Northern soldiers shot Colt revolvers. Southern soldiers used LaMat revolvers. LaMats fired nine shots before they needed to be reloaded.

WEAPON FACT

Soldiers on horseback used revolvers so they could easily ride and shoot at the same time.

Colt revolver

LaMat revolver

Blades worked well in hand-to-hand fighting. **Bayonets** fit onto the ends of rifles. Soldiers on horseback sliced enemies with **sabers**.

bayonet — a blade attached to the end of a rifle

saber — a sword with a slightly curved blade

SMALL ARMS

Colt revolver

LaMat revolver

Spencer repeating rifle

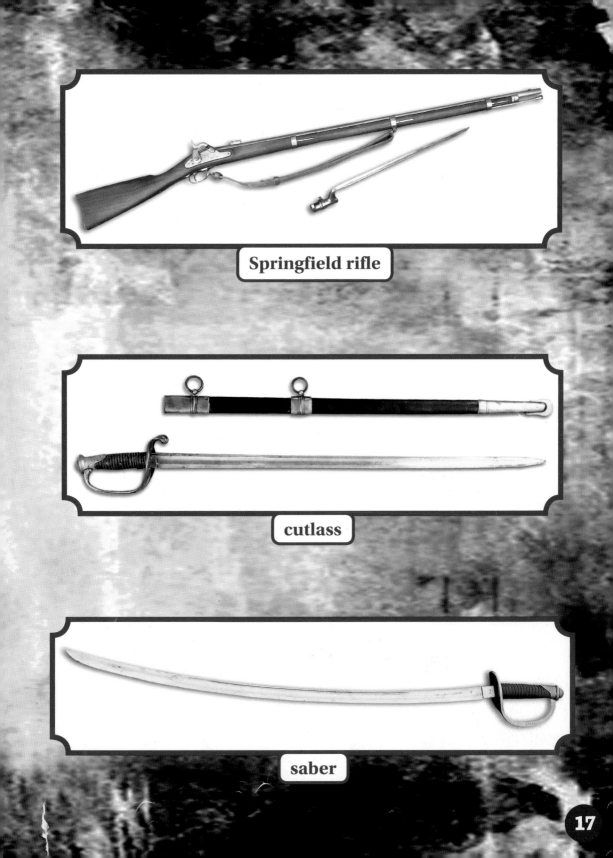

Springfield rifle

cutlass

saber

THE BIG GUNS

Large weapons were called **artillery**. They did the most damage. A cannon shot could kill 10 soldiers or more.

artillery — cannons and other large guns

cannon

The Gatling gun was one of the first machine guns. Soldiers turned a handle to fire the gun. It had six barrels. Each barrel fired 100 bullets per minute.

WEAPON FACT

Richard Gatling invented the Gatling gun. He improved the gun over several years. A later model had 10 barrels.

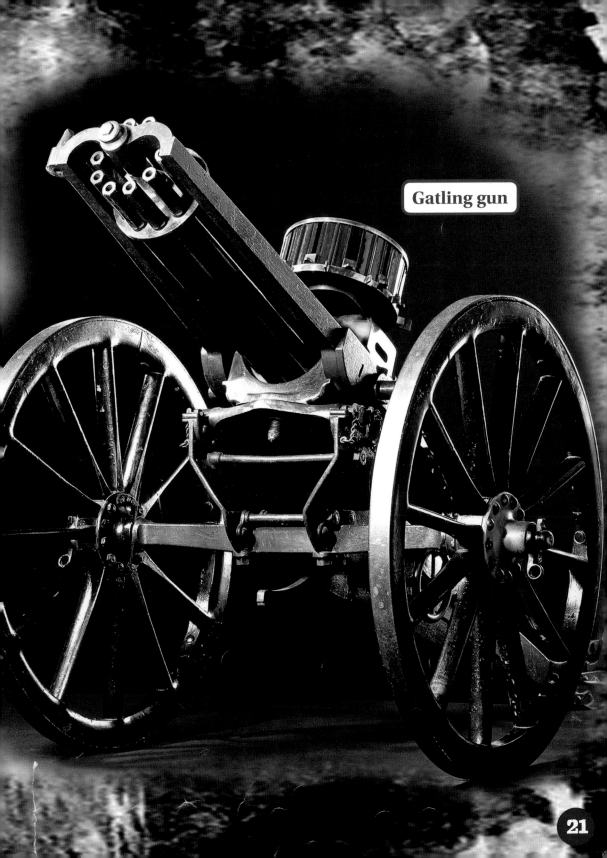

Gatling gun

Howitzer

Both sides fired the Howitzer. This cannon could hit targets 1 mile (1.6 kilometers) away. Soldiers also threw **grenades** and launched **mortar** shells at enemies.

grenade — a small bomb that can be thrown

mortar — a short cannon that shoots small explosive shells

LARGER WEAPONS

12-pound cannon

32-pound cannon

30-pound Parrot rifle

Ordinance rifle

Gatling gun

13-inch mortar

cannonball

grenade

LINE OF DEFENSE

Both armies tried to slow enemy travel. They built barriers called **chevaux-de-frise** across main roads. These barriers were made of angled wooden spikes.

chevaux-de-frise (shuh-VOH-duh-freez) — a French word for barriers made of spikes criss-crossed over a wooden frame; the singular form is cheval-de-frise.

chevaux-de-frise

Soldiers had little defense against powerful cannons and rifles. Before the Civil War ended, 620,000 Americans had died.

WEAPON FACT

About 50,000 soldiers ended up killed, wounded, or missing in the battle of Gettysburg in 1863.

GLOSSARY

artillery (ar-TI-luhr-ee) — cannons and other large guns used during battles

bayonet (BAY-uh-nuht) — a long metal blade attached to the end of a musket or rifle

cannon (KAN-uhn) — a large gun that fires large explosive shells

chevaux-de-frise (shuh-VOH-duh-freez) — a French word for barriers made of spikes that are criss-crossed over a wooden frame; the singular form is cheval-de-frise.

grenade (gruh-NAYD) — a small bomb that can be thrown or launched

mortar (MOR-tur) — a short cannon that shoots small, explosive shells

range (RAYNJ) — the maximum distance ammunition can travel to reach its target

rifle (RYE-fuhl) — a powerful gun that is fired from the shoulder

saber (SAY-bur) — a sword with a curved blade and one cutting edge

slavery (SLAY-vur-ee) — the owning of other people; slaves are forced to work without pay.

READ MORE

DeFord, Deborah H. *The Civil War.* Wars that Changed American History. Milwaukee: World Almanac Library, 2007.

Lieurance, Suzanne. *Weapons and Strategies of the Civil War.* The American Civil War. Berkeley Heights, N.J.: MyReportLinks.com Books, 2004.

Westwell, Ian. *The Civil War.* Wars Day By Day. Redding, Conn.: Brown Bear Books, 2009.

INTERNET SITES

FactHound offers a safe, fun way to find Internet sites related to this book. All of the sites on FactHound have been researched by our staff.

Here's how:
1. Visit *www.facthound.com*
2. Choose your grade level.
3. Type in this book ID **1429619686** for age-appropriate sites. You may also browse subjects by clicking on letters, or by clicking on pictures and words.
4. Click on the **Fetch It** button.

FactHound will fetch the best sites for you!

INDEX